The Complete Ave Maria

Includes two celebrated settings by Franz Schubert and J.S. Bach/Charles Gounod

Contents

by Franz Schubert

With Piano Accompaniment:

With Organ Accompaniment:

by J.S. Bach/Charles Gounod

With Piano Accompaniment:

With Organ Accompaniment:

 **Hal Leonard Publishing Corporation**

7777 West Bluemound Road P.O. Box 13819 Milwaukee, WI 53213

ISBN 0-7935-1196-8

Ave Maria

Low Voice with Piano

Franz Schubert

Ave Maria

Medium Voice with Piano

Franz Schubert

Sehr langsam (Molto adagio)

pp

(With Pedal)

sim.

A - ve Ma - ri - a!
A - ve Ma - ri - a!

a! gra - ti - a ple -
a! Ma - ter De -

Ave Maria

High Voice with Piano

Franz Schubert

Ave Maria

Low Voice with Organ

Swell: Flute 8' (Sustain), Harp
Great: Soft 8', 4', String Celeste
Pedal: Soft 16'

Franz Schubert
Transcribed by Phillip Keveren

A - ve Ma - ri -
A - ve Ma - ri -

a!
a!

dim.

Ave Maria

Medium Voice with Organ

Swell: Flute 8' (Sustain), Harp
Great: Soft 8', 4', String Celeste
Pedal: Soft 16'

Franz Schubert
Transcribed by Phillip Keveren

Ave Maria

High Voice with Organ

Swell: Flute 8' (Sustain), Harp
Great: Soft 8', 4', String Celeste
Pedal: Soft 16'

Franz Schubert
Transcribed by Phillip Keveren

Ave Maria

Piano Solo

Franz Schubert
Trancribed by Phillip Keveren

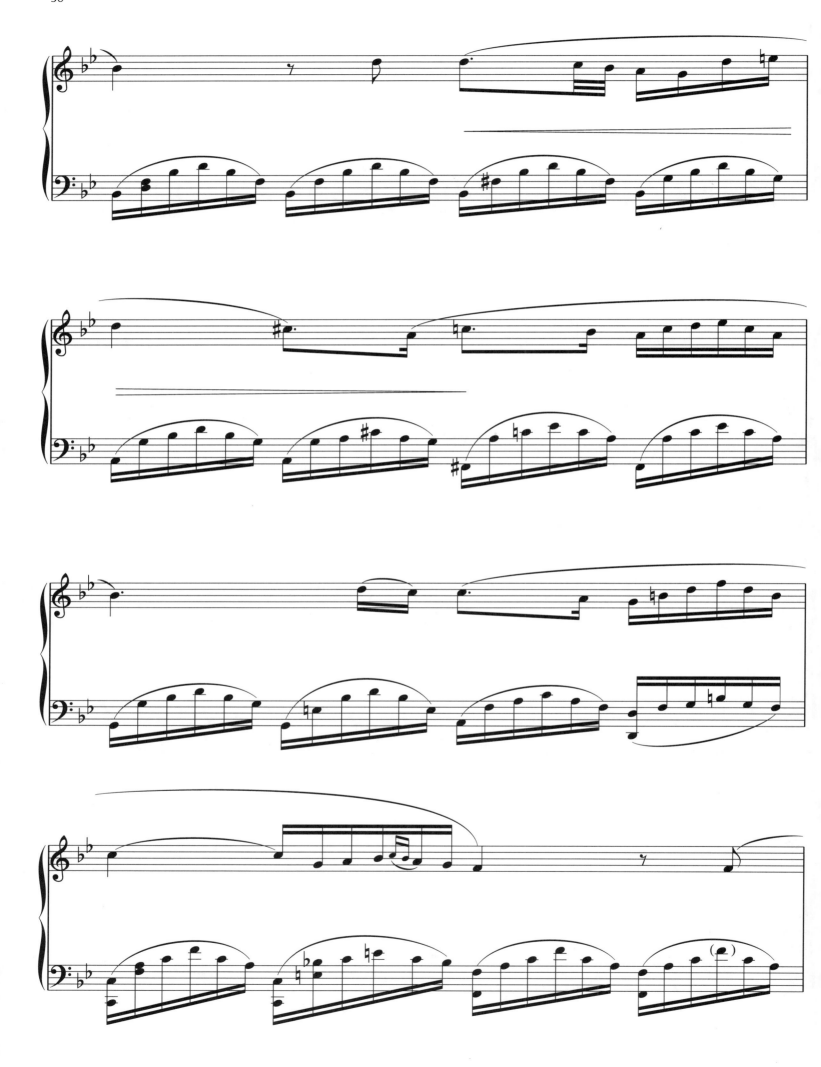

Ave Maria

Organ Solo

Swell: Solo Reed (Prepare Flutes 8′ 4′ 2′, String 8′)
Great: Soft 8′ 4′
Pedal: Soft 16′

Franz Schubert
Trancribed by Phillip Keveren

Flute 8' 4' 2', String 8'

Ave Maria
(adapted from "Prelude in C" by J.S. Bach)

Low Voice with Piano

Charles Gounod

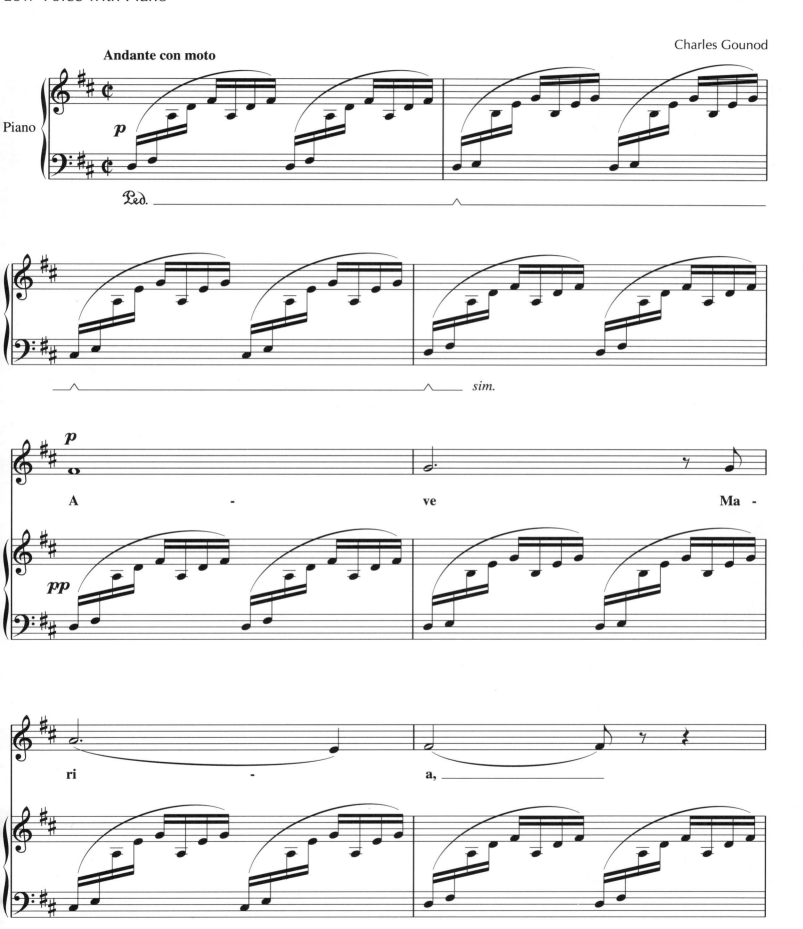

e - ri - bus et _____ be - ne -

dic - tus fruc - tus _____

ven - tris _____ tu - i Je -

sus. _____ Sanc - ta Ma -

Ave Maria
(adapted from "Prelude in C" by J.S. Bach)

Medium Voice with Piano

Charles Gounod

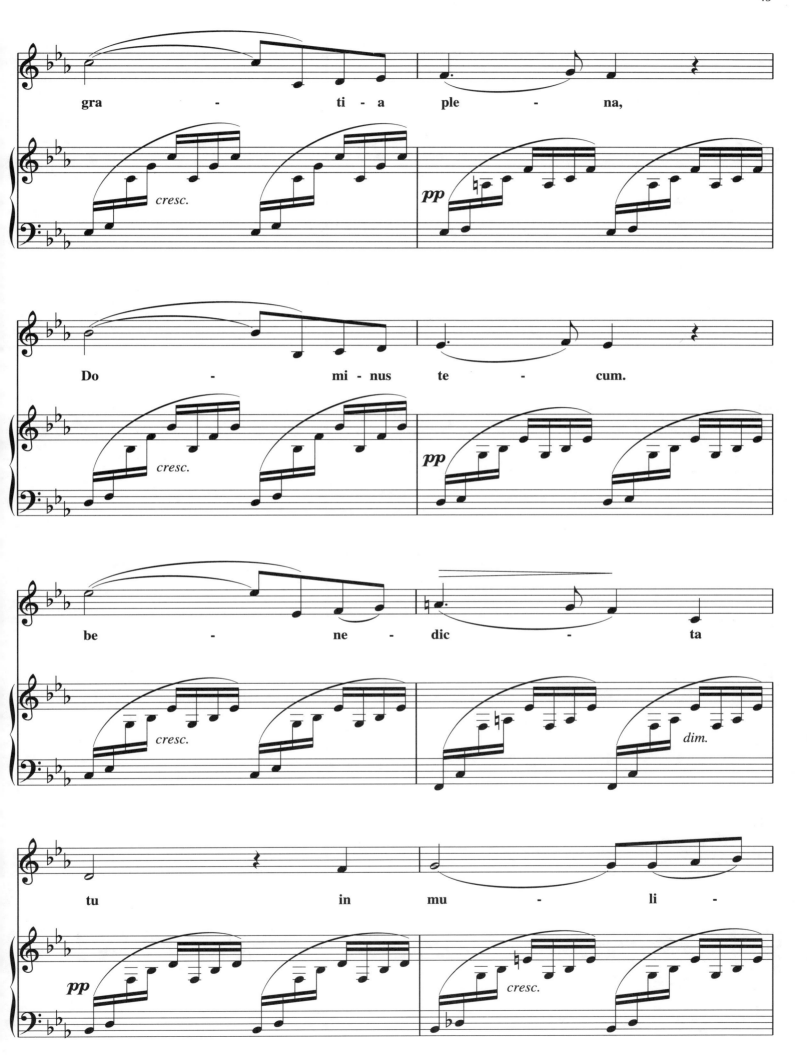

Ave Maria
(adapted from "Prelude in C" by J.S. Bach)

High Voice with Piano

Charles Gounod

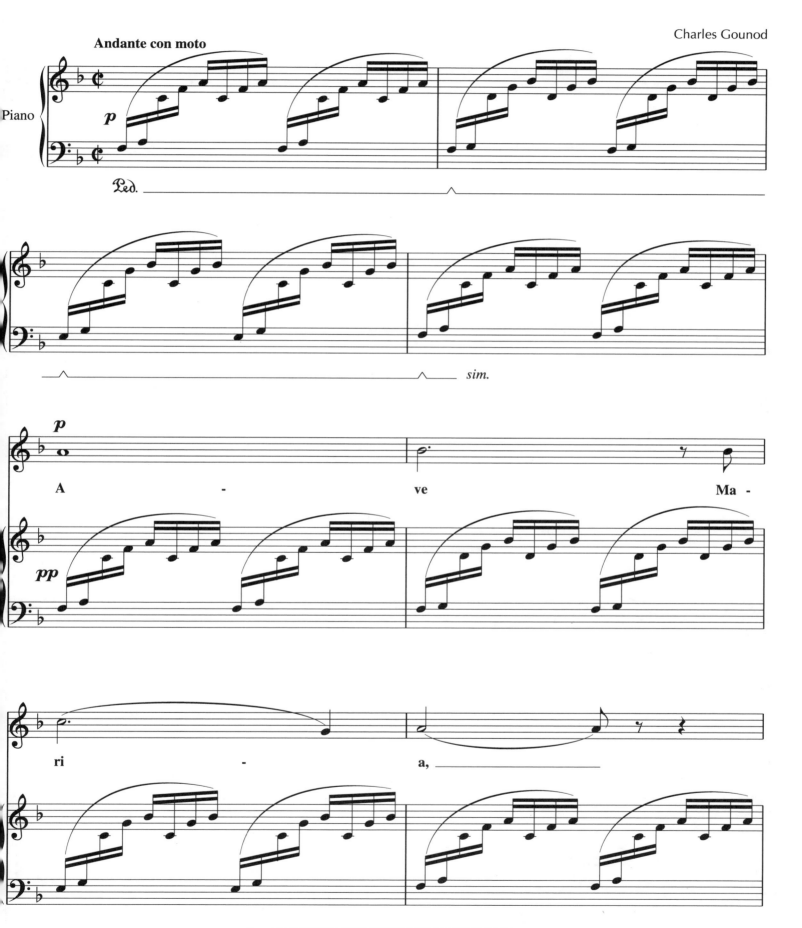

Ave Maria
(adapted from "Prelude in C" by J.S. Bach)

Low Voice with Organ

Swell: Flute 8', 4', String Celeste
Great: Flute 8' (Sustain), Harp
Pedal: Soft 16'

Charles Gounod
Transcribed by Phillip Keveren

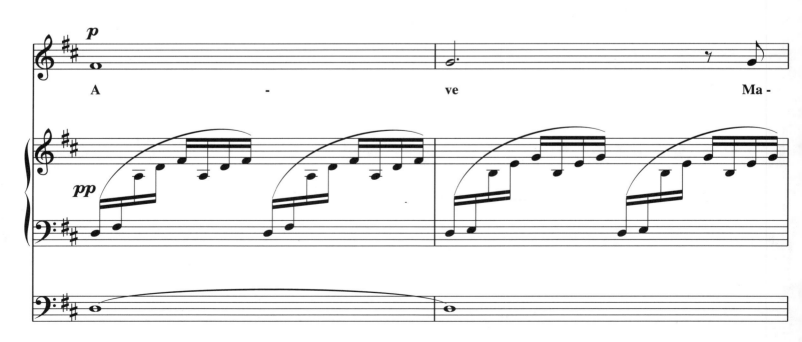

dic - tus fruc - tus

ven - tris tu - i Je -

sus. Sanc - ta Ma - ri - a,

cresc.

dim.

Gt.

Sw.

Ave Maria
(adapted from "Prelude in C" by J.S. Bach)

Medium Voice with Organ

Swell: Flute 8', 4', String Celeste
Great: Flute 8' (Sustain), Harp
Pedal: Soft 16'

Charles Gounod
Transcribed by Phillip Keveren

Manuals

Pedal

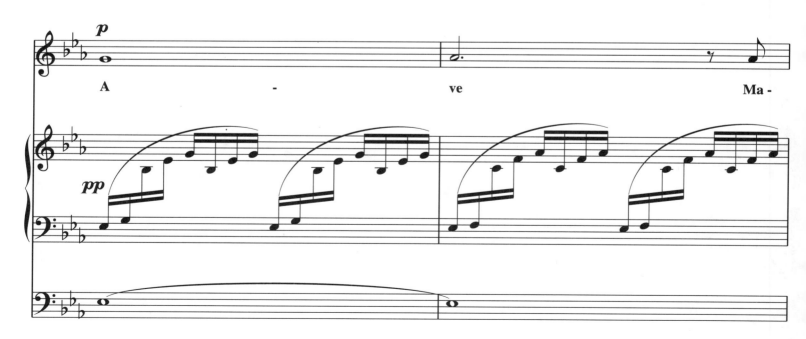

A - ve Ma-

be - ne - dic - ta

tu ____ in mu - li -

e - ri - bus et _____ be - ne -

ho - ra, in ho - ra ___ mor - tis ___ nos - trae, ___

A - men!

dim.

p

poco rit.

A - men!

pp

poco rit.

Ave Maria
(adapted from "Prelude in C" by J.S. Bach)

High Voice with Organ

Swell: Flute 8', 4', String Celeste
Great: Flute 8' (Sustain), Harp
Pedal: Soft 16'

Charles Gounod
Transcribed by Phillip Kerveren

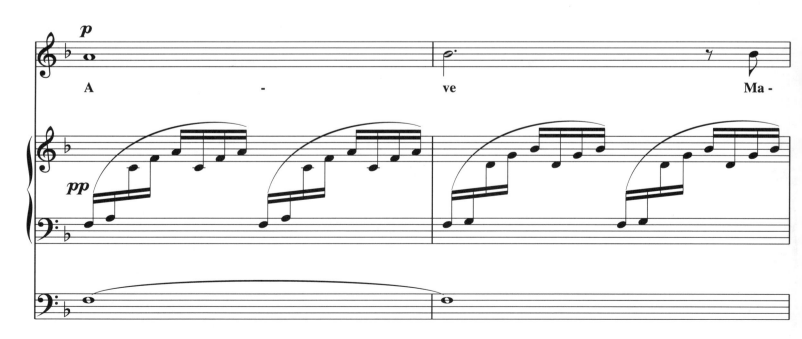

dic - tus fruc - tus _____ ven - tris _____ tu - i Je - sus. _____ Sanc - ta Ma - ri - a,

cresc.

dim.

p

Gt.

Sw.

p

Ave Maria
(adapted from "Prelude in C" by J.S. Bach)

Piano Solo

Charles Gounod
Transcribed by Todd Lowry

Ave Maria
(adapted from "Prelude in C" by J.S. Bach)

Organ Solo

Swell: Strings 8'
Great: Flutes 8', 2 2/3', 2', Tremulat
Pedal: Flutes 16', 8'

Charles Gounod
Transcribed by Todd Lowry

cresc.

crtesc.

mf

mf

p

mp

p

mp

*T*he traditional Latin text of the "Ave Maria" prayer:

Ave Maria, gratia plena; Dominus tecum,
benedicta tu in mulieribus, et benedictus
fructus ventris tui, Jesus.

Sancta Maria, Mater Dei
ora pro nobis peccatoribus,
nunc et in hora mortis nostrae. Amen.

*T*he singer's translation of the Latin text of the "Ave Maria" prayer:

Ave Maria! You are highly favored, God is with thee.
Blessed, blessed are you, are you above all women,
Blessed be your offspring,
Blessed be your son, the son of God, the Lord most high!

Holy Maria! Holy Maria, Maria!
Pray, oh, pray for us, for us wretched sinners,
Now and at the hour of our death,
at the hour of our death. Amen.

*T*he "Ave Maria" prayer as it is used by present-day Catholics:

Hail Mary, full of grace! The Lord is with thee
Blessed art thou among women,
and blessed is the fruit of thy womb, Jesus.

Holy Mary, Mother of God, pray for us sinners,
now and at the hour of our death. Amen.